Addictions Recovery Devotional Workbook:

52 Weeks of Biblically-based Practical Exercises for Strength and Healing

James E. Phelan, MSW, Psy.D

Copyright © 2018
James E. Phelan

Published by:
Practical Application Publications
All rights reserved.

ISBN-10: 0977977374
ISBN-13: 978-0977977376

No portion of this book may be reproduced in any manner without the permission of the author or publisher.

ClipArt, Copyright © 2004 Microsoft Corporation

Unless otherwise stated, all Scripture is cited from:

Holy Bible, New International Version®, NIV® Copyright ©1973, 1978, 1984, 2011 by Biblica, Inc.®. All rights reserved worldwide.

To all my clients who give me purpose each day. To my family for loving and supporting me, and for all their sacrifices. A special thanks to Darla for helping me with this project.

About the Author

James E. Phelan received his doctorate degree in Psychology (Psy.D) from California Southern University, his master's degree in Social Work (MSW) from Marywood University, and diploma in Biblical Studies from Liberty University. He is a Board Certified Diplomate in Clinical Social Work (BCD) and an Internationally Certified Alcohol and Drug Abuse Counselor (ICADC). He is also a Veteran having served the U.S. Army, U.S. Army Reserves, and the U.S. Air Force.

Introduction

The *Addictions Recovery Devotional Workbook* provides practical applications in a way that can enhance your life through the Bible. God's Word offers an array of examples that can help us in our life's domination struggles. Each week this workbook offers a segment from Scripture, then drawing on that Scripture, makes a way for which you can apply it to your life in a way that can help transform change. Daily application can be achieved through doing, talking, thinking, reading or writing. Each one ends in a prayer that is meant to connect you and God in a way that reflects practical application. Each one offers new opportunities for advancing your life and addresses key issues necessary for recovery. Please carve out some time to devoted to your recovery and healing in a way that brings you closer to God and those who mean so much to you. It is my secure desire that this workbook will help you in your journey to do so.

"Jesus [taught and proclaimed] the good news…and heal[ed] every disease and sickness among the people."

- Matthew 4:23

Symbols

Look for one these symbols in each weekly practical devotional:

 Think about it!

 Do it!

 Talk about it!

 Write it!

 Read it!

Week 1: Renewal

Therefore, if anyone is in Christ, he is a new creation. The old has passed away; behold, the new has come. (2 Corinthians 5:17)

APPLICATION

The New Year is a time of renewal. The word *renewal* means to restore or become new spiritually. Be renewed by taking a short walk in God's Word for encouragement of God's promises. Be well, knowing renewal is God's gift to us. This week use the journal/workspace to process how the idea in each assigned Scripture can be applied to your recovery each particular day.

Read:

Day 1 - Isaiah 57:10

Day 2 - Romans 12:2

Day 3 - Titus 3:5

Day 4 - 2 Corinthians 4:16

Day 5 - Psalms 103:5

Day 6 - Psalms 51:10

Day 7 - Colossians 3:10

PRAYER

Lord, renew my heart and mind as I begin this New Year. Lead me to new pathways and opportunities.

Journal/Workspace

Week 2: Acceptance

 *But Barnabas took him and brought him to the apostles. He told them how Saul, on his journey, had seen the LORD and that the LORD had spoken to him, and how in Damascus he had preached fearlessly in the name of Jesus. So Saul stayed with them and moved about freely in Jerusalem, speaking boldly in the name of the LORD. (Acts 9:27-28)*

APPLICATION

The apostles, who were Jesus' closest friends, were somewhat skeptical about the sincerity of Saul's change of heart. But, you really can't blame them, can you? After all, a few weeks prior to that, Saul threatened to kill them and in fact had killed some of their friends for no other reason other than the fact that they acknowledged Jesus as the Savior.

It is likely you, too, will experience a bit of resistance from others—especially in the first year or so of your recovery. Those who have been affected by your past may find it difficult to accept that you are truly in recovery. Their hesitation will undoubtedly be a bit hurtful, but don't let it get you down. Be like Saul—boldly and shamelessly proving that you are no longer the person you were before. Show them that person no longer exists.

Think about the following and record your thoughts in your journal/workspace.

Q: Who has been hesitant to accept that my recovery is sincere? Why?

Q: What actions can I take to show them that I am sincere and can change.

Q: Who has been the most accepting of me since I have started the road to recovery?

Q: What can I do to express my gratitude for their trust in me?

Q: Acceptance will take time; trust can follow. But, what steps can you take to rebuild?

PRAYER

Father in Heaven, Give me the strength to not let anyone's doubts about me act as a roadblock in my life. Let me be bold in all ways that make me a better person for you. In Jesus' name I pray, amen.

Journal/Workspace

Week 3: Mentoring

So Elisha left him and went back. He took his yoke of oxen and slaughtered them. He burned the plowing equipment to cook the meat and gave it to the people, and they ate. Then he set out to follow Elijah and become his attendant. (1 Kings 19:21)

APPLICATION

Elijah was completely sold-out for God. So much so, in fact, that God sent Elisha to learn from Elijah…to be mentored by Elijah so that the legacy of his faith and obedience could be passed on to others. Elisha was willing and grateful to be mentored by Elijah; making the most of each and every day they spent together.

A mentor is a valuable resource. Having someone you admire and respect and who genuinely cares about your wellbeing, to learn from and confide in, can make all the difference in the world when it comes to sustained recovery. Finding a mentor, one who can relate and has walked the talk (in 12-step programs we call this a sponsor) can help you in the recovery process.

Take the time this week to answer these questions to help you in choosing someone to mentor you.

Q: Who are three people you most admire and respect because of their Christian attitude and lifestyle?

Q: What is it about them that make you feel this way?

Q: What would you like to learn and how would you like to grow as a result of being mentored by one of these people?

Q: Choose one of the people from your list. Contact them and ask them to serve as your mentor.

For an insightful article* on choosing a Christian sponsor, see:
http://newlifespiritrecovery.com/how-to-choose-a-christian-sponsor/

PRAYER

Father, I am in need of someone to help me grow and mature in my relationship with you and as a person. Give me the courage to ask someone to help me and please lay it on their heart to say yes. In the name of Jesus I pray, amen.

* Articles suggested are for educational purposes available on the public domain, the author does not necessarily endorse their writers and affiliations

Journal/Workspace

Week 4: Family

God sets the lonely in families, he leads out the prisoners with singing…." (Psalms 68:6)

APPLICATION

Geographically, I live far away from most of my family. But, whenever we are together I always get a sense of connectedness and in no way do I feel alone. In contrast, when I depart this situation I always feel a deep sense of void. Family should be a place of refuge and a harbor of safety. For some, family can be painful. Some family members are estranged from one another. Whatever the situation, loneliness can exist. God did not intend us to be alone. In the beginning God did not want Adam to be alone so he created Eve. This is reminiscent of our human need for connectedness.

It is in family that we can be freed from loneliness. If your family is unavailable to you, make it a point to create another family of which you can be a part of.

In this exercise:

1) Talk to someone about family. Share with them the details about your family and ask them to share theirs. This person should be someone you trust and who is safe so you can open up and be real.

2) Seek out someone in your family that you have not been connected to in a while. Plan an event or activity in which you can spend some time together. If this is not geographically feasible then do this remote through the cell phone, internet or perhaps through the use of a media outlet such as Face time or Skype. Talk about things you have not talked about before or things you have not talked about in a while opening up new pathways to connect and regenerate the relationship.

And/or: Plan an event with family. Take note of the feelings of connection and when you depart take notice of any loneliness. Afterward think about the experience and reflect on how family blesses you and how you bless them.

PRAYER

Father, give me the strength to open up to my family, to make any amends needed and to set a course that eliminate any loneness that has set in.

Journal/Workspace

Week 5: Accountability

How can a young person stay on the path of purity? By living according to your Word. (Psalm 119:9)

APPLICATION

"By living according to your word."—it really is that simple…and that hard all at the same time.

It is simple in the fact that God doesn't beat around the bush. His Word, the Bible, clearly states his commands and his expectations for us as his children. Thanks to the fact that we are sinful by nature, however, it isn't always easy for us to obey those commands and meet those expectations. There is something you can do to help you stay on track, though. You can ask a couple of your closest Christian friends to be your accountability partners. Accountability partners are people who encourage you to keep God's commands. They pray for you, fellowship with you, and love you enough to tell you the truth.

Accountability partners use the Bible as the basis for their words and actions—both those that are uplifting as well the ones that reprove and call attention to sins that need to be repented from and confessed to God. Even Jesus had an inner-circle of friends. From the twelve he had three—Peter, James, and John, who were closer to him than the rest. No, Jesus didn't need anyone to hold him accountable because he was perfect. But he *did* need them to encourage him, pray with him, fellowship with him, and serve with him.

Remember, though, the ultimate accountability partner is Jesus and his Word. Read it. Live by it. Share it. Ask one or two of your closest Christian friends if they will be your accountability partner(s). Commit to praying for each other daily, checking in with each other at least three times a week, be accessible to one another, and set aside time to meet together for fellowship at least once a month.

PRAYER

LORD, I know the Bible is the ultimate accountability partner, but I ask that you give me the courage to ask others to help me with accountability. In your name I pray, amen.

Journal/Workspace

Week 6: Unconditional Love

 *Love is patient, love is kind. It does not envy, it does not boast, it is not proud. It is not rude, it is not self-seeking. It is not easily angered, it keeps no record of wrongs. Love does not delight in evil but rejoices with the truth. It always protects, always trusts, always hopes, always perseveres. (1 Corinthians 13:4-7)*

APPLICATION

Our lives are surrounded by conditions. We have them at work, school and everywhere. But what about love? Can we really love without conditions? Like in 1 Corinthians can we "keep no records of wrong"? Can we be so patient that we are not angered? It's easy to say, "I love you", but it's harder to say "I love you unconditionally".

What does it take to love unconditionally? It means, looking past the exterior of a person, and instead looking at their heart, their inner self. Unconditional love cannot be based upon one's performance or it wouldn't be unconditional.

Therefore, it must be based on the intrinsic worth of the person. To be honest, God's love was unconditional for the worth of His people, but not necessarily for their behavior. God has placed many conditions for conduct. God hates sin, but loves the sinner.

So, how can we honestly love others for who they are on the inside, regardless of what they may have done on the outside that we don't like?

In this practical application exercise, think about the people in your life. Ask yourself what you see of them on the inside. Does this differ from what you see on the outside? Next, allow yourself to embrace the thoughts of loving those people regardless of what they may do or have done, rather allow yourself to love them for who they are inside as a people in need of God's love and forgiveness.

PRAYER

Dear Lord, allow me an open heart to love others for who they are on the inside, needy for love, rather than on the outside, humans who have fallen from grace and need your salvation. Let me be the light which points to your redemptive love.

Journal/Workspace

Week 7: Patience

 *Brothers and sisters, as an example of patience in the face of suffering, take the prophets who spoke in the name of the Lord." (James 5:10; James 5:7-12)*

APPLICATION

James asked the reader to think about the patience of others in doing so to establish grounding for ourselves. Job is one example. Even though Job had opportunity to lose his patience considering all that went wrong in his life, he kept faithful and would not swear against the Lord. In the end, God blessed him immensely.

Think about what James 5:7-12 says. Four basic elements for us to think about are found in this scripture: Waiting, not grumbling, perseverance, and not swearing. Think about it. It's clear that when we get impatient we find it hard to wait, we often grumble, and swear. We feel like giving up! How easy is it to grumble when someone does not hurrying in the manner we wish? How easy then is it to swear or to just give up on that person?

In thinking about these, ask yourselves how you can exercise patience throughout this week and into the future. Use the following questions to help guide you:

Q: Who am I most impatient with? How can I be more patient with them this week?

Q: What can I do when I start to grumble as I grow inpatient?

Q: When I am struggling with waiting, how can I think about scripture and gear myself toward perseverance?

PRAYER

Patience is an example you held for all of us, oh Lord. Please help me to think about the patience of others such as Job and of your ultimate patience as I strive to seek this in my own life so I may be more complete and free. In the name of Jesus, amen.

Journal/Workspace

Week 8: Boundaries

We, however, will not boast beyond proper limits, but will confine boasting to the sphere of service God himself has assigned to us...." (2 Corinthians 10:13)

APPLICATION

What does it mean to "boast" in "proper limits"? In general, boasting is expressing too much pride in yourself or in something you have, have done, or are connected to in some way. Instead of boasting about ourselves and what we've done, let's boast about God and what He has done for us. This is the boundary God has set for us (the "proper limit"). When we take the focus of ourselves and place it on God, He gets the rightful glory. It is then that the lost can see His light.

Read the following selected passages on examples of how others have confined themselves to the service of God:

Day 1: Matthew 1:20   Day 2: Acts 9:17-18

Day 3: Acts 14:1   Day 4: Luke 5:10

Day 5: Genesis 18:19   Day 6: Matthew 27:55-56

Day 7: 1 Samuel 16:14

PRAYER

Lord may you be given all the glory. Help me to learn to stay in my limits and boundaries. May the focus be off of me and on to you where it belongs. In this I pray the lost will find you as you steal the show!

Journal/Workspace

Week 9: Persistence

Therefore, since we are surrounded by such a great cloud of witnesses, let us throw off everything that hinders and the sin that so easily entangles. And let us run with perseverance the race marked out for us, fixing our eyes on Jesus, the pioneer and perfecter of faith. For the joy set before Him he endured the cross, scorning its shame, and sat down at the right hand of the throne of God. (Hebrews 12:1-2)

APPLICATION

The passage in Hebrews 12:1-2 is a good example of persistence. The example of how Jesus endured the cross gives a clear indication of such. In doing so, he laid aside everything else in order to please His Father. The cross was God's plan to save our sins and we should be relieved he endured the cross on our behalf. Hebrews tells us to lay aside every weight and run with endurance as if we were running a marathon.

What weight do you need to lay aside? What is holding you back from moving forward? In this practical exercise list all the weights that hold you back. Next, list a plan for how you can lay aside this weight.

Example:

<u>My weight:</u>

<u>I still hold a grudge against my friend.</u>

<u>My Plan:</u>

<u>I will forgive my friend today, writing him a letter telling him so.</u>

PRAYER

Lord, I have allowed a heavy weight to hold me back from running after you. I have been bogged down and it hurts. Please give me the strength to move forward and activate a plan. In your name I pray, amen.

Journal/Workspace

Week 10: Witnessing

Therefore go and make disciples of all nations, baptizing them in the name of the Father and of the Son and of the Holy Spirit, and teaching them to obey everything I have commanded you. (Matthew 28:19-20a)

APPLICATION

There is really no room for misunderstanding or misinterpretation in today's verses is there? Jesus' last words on earth tell us to go, reach the lost, and baptize them. But, Jesus doesn't just stop there. He explicitly tells us what we are to teach complete obedience to EVERYTHING he had taught while here on earth.

When we do that—when we live obediently in Christ—our words as well as our actions are a witness to others for Jesus Christ. They see Jesus in us. They hear Jesus in us. They experience Jesus through us.

This week do at least two of the following:

*Post a favorite Bible verse on your social media accounts.

*Ask a non-Christian friend or family member to church.

*Write, "I pray you have a wonderful day" on a napkin or piece of paper and leave it for your waitress/waiter.

*Give a homeless person a gift card for food and a devotional book.

*Tell someone how you came to know Jesus and what he has done in your life.

PRAYER

LORD, help me be a witness and positive influence to someone who doesn't yet know you. Help those I meet this week see you in me. In your name I pray, amen.

Journal/Workspace

Week 11: Recovery

Therefore, if anyone is in Christ, he is a new creation; the old has gone, the new has come! (2 Corinthians 5:17)

APPLICATION

In many circles, recovery means to return to the so-called "normal" status quo, or a "process" of change. But, for Christ recovery is not a return to something former, or a process, rather it means that the old is actually gone and an anew has transpired. When Saul was filled with the Holy Spirit he did regain his physical strength, but he was never the same man again. He was changed. Saul, once a prosecutor, became Paul, one of God's most dedicated apostles.

This week use the following daily devotional reading plan that embodies this topic:

Day 1: Acts 9:17-18

Day 2: Galatians 6:15

Day 3: Hebrews 8:13

Day 4: 1 Peter 1:3

Day 5: Mark 2:22

Day 6: 1 Corinthians 5:6-8

Day 7: 1 Corinthians 15:52

PRAYER

Help me Lord not to recover in the way the world would see it, but as you see it: A transformation, an actual new change, not a process of a going back to the old self.

Journal/Workspace

Week 12: Forgiveness

... forgive your brothers the sins and the wrongs they committed in treating you... (Genesis 50:17)

APPLICATION

Joseph's brothers did some pretty nasty things to him. They plotted against him, sold him into slavery, and imprisoned him. After all of this, Joseph found it in his heart to forgive them. He also promised he would help them and their families.

Forgiveness is writing off any debt you may feel is owed. You can tell someone they hurt you, but not necessarily expect them to pay you back. In many cases they could not pay back for all the pain they have caused anyway.

Releasing the burden of the debt of those who cannot pay you back might help you in your journey of recovery. For those who have emotionally hurt you, forgive them. For those who may owe you something material, cancel the debt. This can set your heart free of harboring resentments and anger.

Sometimes it is appropriate to exercise the act of forgiveness by telling those may have hurt you in person. Sometimes writing it and sending it (or not) may be necessary if the person is no longer alive or it may not be appropriate to do so. Whatever the case, the act of forgivingness is important for you. Remember, forgiveness sets your heart free of harboring resentments and anger.

Consider these questions as you move forward toward forgiveness:

Q: Who do I need to forgive?

Q: How and when will I do this?

Q: Who can support me in this process?

Q: What good will I take from this?

PRAYER

I am in need of forgiveness and so is my brother, dear Lord. I ask for forgiveness. Please give me the strength I need to forgive others so I no longer hold this burden

Journal/Workspace

Week 13: Grace

But he said to me, "My grace is sufficient for you, for my power is made perfect in weakness." Therefore I will boast all the more gladly about my weaknesses, so that Christ's power may rest on me. (2 Corinthians 12:9)

APPLICATION

Nothing we do on our own is enough to get us into heaven. It is only by the grace and mercy of God that we have the opportunity to be there for all eternity.

We are weak. But grace comes from God and gives us the strength we need, strength we cannot get on our own. In other words, it is by God's grace we live and have our being. The Bible tells us to "Be strengthened by the grace that is in Jesus Christ" (2 Timothy 2:1) for "it is good for the heart to be strengthened by grace." (Hebrews 13:9)

Talk to your accountability partner or trusted Christian friend about grace and how it provides you the strength you need to gain recovery.

PRAYER

LORD, Thank you for your grace. I ask now for help in giving up all of who I am to become all of who you created me to be. In your name I pray, amen.

Journal/Workspace

Week 14: Remember

...and when he had given thanks, he broke it and said, "This is my body, which is for you; do this in remembrance of me. (1 Corinthians 11:24)

APPLICATION

Communion is a time of remembrance of the sacrifice Jesus made on the cross for our sins. 1 Corinthians 11:24 talks about the cup, which is the blood of Jesus.

Communion is truly a special event—something we must be careful of not taking for granted or turning into a ritual or habit. But, how do we do that? Drain your mind of anything but Jesus and envision the pain and suffering he went through on your behalf; let this bring you to a state of humility.

Read John 19:16-18: "So the soldiers took charge of Jesus. Carrying his own cross, he went out to the place of the Skull (which in Aramaic is called Golgotha). There they crucified Him, and with Him two others—one on each side and Jesus in the middle."

Jesus went through all of that...for you!

1) Sometime this week set aside ten or fifteen minutes to have a private and meaningful communion service—just you and God.
2) Decide to be more in-tune to the purpose and significance of the communion service you participate in with your church family. Think of ways you can make sure this happens and do them.

PRAYER

Father, help me remember what communion is all about. Help me never forget just what a privilege it is because of the sacrifice you made on my behalf. In the name of Jesus, the sacrifice for my sins, amen.

Journal/Workspace

Week 15: Astray

If we confess our sins, he is faithful and just and will forgive us our sins and purify us from all unrighteousness. (1 John 1:9)

APPLICATION

A father and son had a serious falling out. The son was upset because he didn't understand why his dad was making a particular decision. There was nothing wrong with what the dad was doing. His son simply didn't 'get it'. The son's lack of understanding caused him to become angry and confrontational. As a result, the two didn't speak for nearly three years. It was only when the father wrote his son a letter saying that forgiveness and moving forward were far more important than any pride either was holding on to, that things changed.

That's what we have to do when we accept Jesus as our Savior. We confess our sins, repent of those sins, and set aside our pride and selfishness so that we can move forward.

What sins do you need to confess and be purified from? Write them down. Be specific. Now read your list to God and ask Him to purify you of these offenses and bring you back to Him.

PRAYER

Father in heaven, I ask that you forgive my sins. Forgive me for (name them). I am sorry and I want you to give me the wisdom I need to not repeat them or let them become habits. Keep me focused on being your faithful child. In Jesus' name I pray, amen.

Journal/Workspace

Week 16: Surrender

Those who know your name trust in you, for you, Lord, have never forsaken those who seek you. (Psalm 9:10)

APPLCIATION

Gideon and his army of 300 fought and won against an army of thousands. But do you know why they were successful? Surrender—Gideon's surrender to God. By trusting God in a seemingly impossible situation, the Israelites experienced victory. They also experienced something else—something even more important. Their faith took a gigantic growth spurt.

It's true God works through us, but it is only when we surrender—when we ride shotgun instead of expecting God to take that seat—that we see and experience the full majesty of our heavenly father.

Read the following verses each day this week and let them make you more submissive to God's will for your life.

Day 1: Matthew 16:24-27

Day 2: James 4:8

Day 3: Romans 12:1

Day 4: 1st Corinthians 6:20

Day 5: Revelation 3:20

Day 6: John 3:30

Day 7: Deuteronomy 28:1

PRAYER

LORD, take away any bit of pride left in me so that I can totally surrender my life to you and make me willing to do your will for my life. In the name of Jesus I pray, amen.

Journal/Workspace

Week 17: Healing

The Centurion replied, Lord, I do not deserve to have you come under my roof. But just say the word, and my servant will be healed." (Matthew 8:7)

APPLICATION

In our pain and infirmities, we may turn to God for instant healing, such as in the case of the Centurion's servant. Jesus can heal immediately for sure. This is evident in his contact with the Centurion and in many other examples within the Bible (continue reading Matthew 8 and 9). It is not our right to be healed, but it is right to ask for it. God's hand of healing is not always as swift as it was with the Centurion's servant. If God does not seem to answer our call for healing, we may complain, or feel as if He doesn't care. But God's plan for our healing is really the act of worship - that is our petition to the Lord, our obedience, and our perseverance. It is in these acts that we will surely see God's true hand placed in our life. The outcome may not be exactly what we invasion, but we will be changed when following Him. Once we take the step to ask for healing, it is then our responsibility to follow Him and accept His will for our lives. That should stand true if even He does not immediately answer our request.

Today, petition the Lord for His hand of healing in at least one area of your life. Make a commitment to follow Him in obedience as you persevere and do not wavier if you don't see immediate results.

PRAYER

Dear Lord, I pray for true healing in my life. I pray that I will remain obedient and preserve in my infirmities, waiting on you for your perfect will.

Journal/Workspace

Week 18: Armor

 *Finally, be strong in the Lord and in his mighty power. Put on the full armor of God, so that you can take your stand against the devil's schemes. (Ephesians 6:10-11)*

APPLICATION

A suit of armor covers the body, is made in such a way that it is nearly impossible to penetrate, and it is worn so that all the major organs of the body are covered/protected.

This is exactly what the armor of God does, too. It covers us from head to toe, is impossible to penetrate (when worn correctly and as a whole), and it covers all our major spiritual 'organs'.

God knows we need his armor in order to fight off our enemy, Satan. God knows that Satan is relentless and a devious schemer. God knows if Satan can't get us to turn on God one way, he'll try different tactics. Satan cannot work if he's not allowed in, though, so be like the Roman soldiers Paul was undoubtedly envisioning as he wrote this. Put on your armor. Wear it daily. Wear it correctly. Wear it because your life depends on it.

1. Read Ephesians 6:10-17 at least once a day ever day this week.

2. Which pieces do you have no problem wearing?

3. Which ones still need to become part of your daily attire?

PRAYER

LORD, make me a solider for your kingdom. Help me be prepared willing to fight every battle Satan brings my way. In your name I pray, amen.

Journal/Workspace

Week 19: Faith

I long to see you so that I may impart to you some spiritual gift to make you strong—that is, that you and I may be mutually encouraged by each other's faith. (Romans 1:11-12)

APPLICATION

While being encouraged by the faith in others our own faith is strengthened. Paul taught us about this concept in his message to the Romans. Paul longed to be around others whose faith was strong. In Romans chapter one he talks about how well known the faithfulness of Romans were at that time and how he longed to be with them (Romans 1:8). He was encouraged by their faith and in turn it strengthened his own. Who among you has strong faith? Are you spending adequate with these people. Ever been around the unfaithful? What happened to you then?

Plan an occasion this week where you are assembled with others who are strong in their faith. Perhaps this would entail attending a faith-based group. Perhaps you could plan a get together with a person, or a few people from your church. Whatever you decide, make sure you share something about your faith and create an open, safe environment where others can share theirs.

PRAYER

Dear Father, let my faith be strong. Allow me to encourage others. Allow me to be with others whose faith I can be encouraged by. Allow us to gather together more frequently so we can lift each other up and further your Kingdom, oh Lord, amen.

Journal/Workspace

Week 20: Authenticity

Let us draw near to God with a sincere heart and with the full assurance that faith brings, having our hearts sprinkled to cleanse us from a guilty conscience and having our bodies washed with pure water. (Hebrews 10:22)

APPLICATION

Active addiction, in a sense, is a running away from authenticity. Addiction is a chase of something other than what is reality. Getting the high is putting yourself in a fantasy, an escape. Being authentic is no longer part of an addict's lifestyle. Addict's elude reality making it hard for others to understand them, let alone help them.

Pretending to be someone you aren't or acting in an insincere manner is never a good thing. Not only are you deceiving others, but you are deceiving yourself, as well. When you pretend or lie about needing help or feeling tempted, you are putting your recovery on the line. When you try to convince yourself and others you don't need God, you are setting yourself up to be distanced from God and from losing the joy and strength that comes from sincere and authentic faith.

Read these daily verses and let them help your faith become more authentic and sincere.

Day 1: Titus 2:7   Day 2: 1Thessalonians 5:21

Day 3: Philippians 2:14   Day 4: Proverbs 17:22

Day 5: Philippians 2:3-5   Day 6: Psalm 139:23-24

Day 7: 1 Peter 5:6

PRAYER

Father in Heaven, Fill me with humility. Let my words and actions be genuine and sincere so that others will know my love for you and my faith in you is authentic. In your son's name I pray, amen.

Journal/Workspace

Week 21: Discouraged

Let us not become weary in doing good, for at the proper time we will reap a harvest if we do not give up. (Galatians 6:9)

APPLICATION

History tells us that President Abraham Lincoln was often discouraged and grieved by the reports he received from the battlefront during the Civil War. But Lincoln did not allow his discouragement to become greater than his will to do what he felt was right.

Hundreds of thousands of American lives were lost in WWII. Those that died did so proudly. They knew that the fight for the freedoms and safety of the world was worth fighting—even if they had to fight to the death.

Peter, John, Stephen, Paul, and others didn't let ridicule, prison, and even torture stand in the way of doing good. They were beaten, starved, shipwrecked, hungry, thirsty, and even murdered because for the sake of winning others to Christ. If anyone were to be discouraged for doing good, it would be them.

In what ways do you tire of doing 'good'? What do you do to rejuvenate yourself; recharging your 'battery' so that you can continue to serve, praise, worship, and grow?

Invite a friend to meet you for lunch of coffee. Talk about some of the issues you both might be facing and how each of you can work without losing faith and without growing weary or discouraged.

PRAYER

God, give me the energy I need to keep working for your kingdom here on earth. Give me determination and help me know that what I do does matter. In your son's name I pray, amen.

Journal/Workspace

Week 22: Wreckage

The God of heaven will give us success. We His servants will start rebuilding.... (Nehemiah 2:19)

APPLICATION

Nehemiah acquired the king's permission to rebuild Jerusalem. The wreckage of the city became Nehemiah's passion. But, Nehemiah could not do it alone. He enlisted the help of others and prayed to God for his serenity. Even in the mist of several groups discouraging them, these faithful servants continued their passion to rebuild the city while being a witness of God's faithfulness.

What wrecks you? My pastor asked that and a few things came to my mind. He furthered that by saying that what wrecks us should then be are passion. Our passion can help lead to solution!

Wow, God can turn wreckage to a passion toward a solution! That hit deep. How can I get passionate about what wrecks me? It's a challenge indeed. What wrecks you? How can you turn this into a passion towards a solution? Who can you enlist to help share the passion?

PRAYER

Please, Lord help me to become passionate about what wrecks me. Give me the courage to move towards a solution rather than a gripe or complaint, amen.

Journal/Workspace

Week 23: Reality

For since the creation of the world God's invisible qualities—His eternal power and divine nature—have been clearly seen, being understood from what has been made, so that people are without excuse. (Romans 1:20)

APPLICATION

If I were going to paraphrase today's verse it would go something like this: God's miraculous, amazing sense of creativity and his sense of humor can be seen everywhere in nature. So look around. If you are honest with yourself you won't be able to deny God's existence. No one but God could have possibly done all of that and it certainly didn't just happen on its own.

Only God can make every zebra's stripe pattern different. Only God can make just one bird—the woodpecker—with a spring-action bone in its neck to handle the rapid thrusting motions they make with their heads. Only God can create sheep so that each momma knows it's baby's bleating…even when hundreds are all 'talking' at the same time. Only God can create the colorful zinnias and fragrant roses. Only God can bring two organisms together to create a human life.

Read chapters 38 thru 42 of the book of Job, then spend a few minutes in prayerful thanks and praise for the mightiness of our creator, God.

PRAYER

Father, you are the Creator. You are the giver of life. You are the master artist. You are the one true God. Thank you for thinking I am worth your time, energy and love. In Jesus' name I pray, amen.

Journal/Workspace

Week 24: Memories

But Mary treasured up all these things and pondered them in her heart. (Luke 2:19)

APPLICATION

The smell of air dried laundry reminds me of my mom. Our clothes and sheets always smelled like clean, crisp, fresh air. I cannot eat a bite of a fresh tomato without thinking about my grandfather who loved growing them. Every time I hear an "oldies" song, I think of the generations before me.

Smells, tastes, songs, sites...all of these things have a way of bringing our memories out of storage and putting them at the forefront of our minds. There is one, memory, however, that should never be put into storage—the memory of what Jesus did for us through his agonizing death on the cross.

Jesus' death is the reason for the blessed assurance we have of eternity in heaven. It is a memory we should cherish and think on each and every day of our life.

Listen to one spiritual song each day this week with the deliberant intention of allowing it to spark memories of God's intercessions in your life.

PRAYER

God, Thank you for the sweet and special memories I have to hold on to. Help me remember what you and your son have done for me. Help me take the time to make special memories with those I love. In Jesus' name I pray, amen.

Journal/Workspace

Week 25: Honesty

Then Peter said, "Ananias, how is it that Satan has so filled your heart that you have lied to the Holy Spirit and have kept for yourself some of the money you received for the land? (Acts 5:3)

APPLICATION

Lying and deceit breaks the bond of trust two people have with one another. And when trust is broken, it isn't easy to put back together. Super glue… not even "Gorilla Glue" can seem get the job done.

Lying is also something that will eat away at your conscious. One lie leads to another and another and another until you aren't even sure what the truth is. Lies don't last—eventually the truth always comes out. Lies are costly. They can cost you your marriage, your job, your freedom, and possibly even your life. In short, honesty truly is the "best policy" and always will be.

What lies are you living with? Confess them to God and ask Him for the courage to replace them with the truth. Then take a deep breath and confess to those you've been dishonest with and make amends. The truth and the act of humility will set you, and those you deceived, free.

PRAYER

LORD, keep my mouth from speaking lies, spreading gossip, and speaking badly about anyone. Instead, let my mouth speak only what is pleasing to you. In Jesus' name I pray, amen.

Journal/Workspace

Week 26: Freedom

It is for freedom that Christ has set us free. Stand firm, then, and do not let yourselves be burdened again by a yoke of slavery." (Galatians 5:1)

APPLICATION

The 4th of July is a big holiday in America. It represents the birth of a country with principles built on seeking freedom. But freedom without reins can create its own problems. For example, while we may be "free" to go out and buy things, the act of spending can create debt, a form of slavery. Freedom can often lead to burden. In Galatians, Paul is teaching others to stand firm against the temptation to use freedom in a way that can be troublesome. Paul reminds us that God has set us free ultimately, but yet it is our responsibility to maintain ourselves in a way that is firm and righteous. Just because we are "free," we are not completely free to do what we want without consequences.

For this week's exercise complete the inventory and action plan:

<u>Inventory</u>: In what way has your freedom kept you in slavery? What are you a slave to?

<u>Action Plan</u>: If you are a slave to something at this time, ask God to relieve this burden. Using the workspace provided on the next page, write out an action plan, one item each day you can do this week, that includes key people that can help you, tools you need, and specific completion times.

PRAYER

Dear Lord, thank you for the freedom you have provided. I ask that I have the courage to not use my freedom to engage in addictive behaviors; that I no longer be a slave to addiction, so that I may stand firm under your grace and forgiveness, amen.

Journal/Workspace

Week 27: Strength

So do not fear, for I am with you; do not be dismayed, for I am your God. I will strengthen you and help you; I will uphold you with my righteous right hand. (Isaiah 41:10)

APPLICATION

There are different kinds of strength. Physical strength gives us the ability to carry or lift heavy objects. Our endurance level is also a measure of physical strength. Emotional or mental strength allows us to hold up under stress and difficult situations. A strong body or a strong heart and mind—two very different kinds of strength, but in one way they are very much alike. Strength, no matter what kind it is, requires training.

Strength training for the body comes through repetitious practice and training. Running drills before running a race, swinging that golf club until you get it right…it's all about consistent practice. Strength training for the heart and mind comes from training yourself to trust in God to give you the encouragement and strength to deal with the stress, grief, and pain life brings each of us in some form(s) or another. Training yourself to have this kind of strength comes through consistent prayer, Bible study, and complete submission to God.

None of us is strong enough to make it through this life on our own. We were created by God to be with God. Relying on God is not a sign of weakness, rather it is our built-in strength mechanism.

<u>Do the following to make today's verse your personal spiritual strength trainer:</u>

1) Write out the words to today's verse on four different note cards. Put one on each of the following places: mirror, nightstand, workspace, car (or lunch bag). This way you will see it and be reminded of it on a regular basis throughout the day.

2) Send yourself an email using today's verse as the body of the email.

PRAYER

Lord, give me the strength to trust you in all things. In Jesus' name, amen.

Journal/Workspace

Week 28: Plans

Commit to the Lord whatever you do, and he will establish your plans.
(Proverbs 16:3)

APPLICATION

Jason had just graduated from college and was beginning his career —something he had wanted to do for a long time. But when the youth minister at his church told Jason he thought he should go into the ministry, Jason left his new job *without* consulting God.

Jason's attempt at youth ministry was a disaster! He was miserable. His wife was miserable. The young people he was supposed to minister to were miserable. So Jason and his wife moved back to their home state to pick up the pieces and move forward. This time, though, they spent several days praying; listening for the answers they knew God would provide. Today Jason and his wife are proud parents and are happy in their chosen fields. They are very involved in their church—but in ways that they feel led by God to be.

Read the verses for each day of the coming week and use them to help you discover God's will for your life.

Day 1: Proverbs 21:5   Day 2: Psalm 37:5

Day 3: John 14:26   Day 4: James 1:19-20

Day 5: Matthew 6:33   Day 6: Proverbs 16:9

Day 7: Jeremiah 29:11

PRAYER

LORD, Show me what you want me to do with my life. Step by step, day by day, give me the wisdom and desire to follow you and you only. In your name I pray, amen.

Journal/Workspace

Week 29: Excuses

Moses said to the Lord, "Pardon your servant, Lord. I have never been eloquent, neither in the past nor since you have spoken to your servant. I am slow of speech and tongue. (Exodus 4:10)

APPLICATION

Moses had all sorts of excuses for God—excuses as to why he shouldn't be the one to lead the Israelites out of Egypt. But God knew better. God knew Moses was perfect for the job and wouldn't take no for an answer.

Have you ever been guilty of making excuses for why you aren't living faithfully and obediently to God? Have you ever been guilty of making excuses for why you 'can't' forgive someone? Don't have time to be the spouse or parent you need to be? Aren't able to keep a promise or fulfill a commitment?

Excuses are an escape hatch from responsibility. Running from responsibility isolates us from where we really need to be. Excuses are really a barrier to recovery. How can we stop making excuses and start living up to our full potential in Christ and allowing Him to work in and through us?

Answer the following questions and challenge your answers to help bring about change:

Q: What excuses have you been making?

Q: Why are you making these excuses?

Q: What excuses are you making for not putting your full faith in Jesus?

Q: Why are you making these excuses?

Q: Ask someone you trust to hold you accountable when excuses keep you from moving forward.

PRAYER

LORD, I don't want to be a person of excuses. I want to be a person of faith and action. Help me do that for you and for me. In Jesus' name I pray, amen.

Journal/Workspace

Week 30: Letting Go

Let all bitterness and wrath and anger and clamor and slander be put away from you, along with all malice. (Ephesians 4:31)

APPLICATION

In the book of Genesis we read the account of twin brothers named Jacob and Esau. Jacob deceived both Esau and their father; causing their father to give Esau's inheritance to Jacob. Years later the two brothers meet face to face. Prior to the meeting Jacob is fearful that Esau will take revenge on him. But when they meet, Esau embraces his brother; telling him that what happened all those years ago didn't matter anymore. He had let go of his anger and resentment and was glad to see his brother again.

Are you holding on to any anger and resentment toward someone? What do you need to let go of? What is still attaching you to your painful past that you need to let go of?

The following TO DO list may not be easy for you, but don't let that stop you. Remember, you have the Holy Spirit to help you:

1: Memorize Matthew 6:14-15. How do you feel knowing this is true?

2: Make a list of all the people you are holding grudges against.

3: Pray for these people and for yourself—to be able to let go of the grudge and anger you have.

4: Go to as many of these people (if possible, or safe to do so) and tell them you are letting go of your anger or resentment. Be willing to be okay with their response, even if it is not the one you would have wanted.

PRAYER

God, Please fill my heart with forgiveness and mercy—the same forgiveness and mercy you extend to me every single day of my life. Help me let go of the things not worth holding on to. In Jesus' name I pray, amen.

Journal/Workspace

Week 31: Enthusiasm

Now finish the work, so your eager willingness to do it may be matched by your completion of it. (2 Corinthians 8:11)

APPLICATION

Have you ever heard someone say that the reason they don't go to church is because the people they know who do go are stern, or even gloomy and dismal-acting? Or have you ever looked around at the people you worshipping with and noticed that they don't look the least bit joyful or spirit-filled? What's up with that?

The joy of the LORD is supposed to be our strength. Complacency and dogmatic ritualism has no place in the hearts and minds of those truly seeking an intimate relationship with the Savior. Those things were for the Pharisees. And you know what Jesus said about them, don't you? He said all the attention they sought (and got) was all the reward they were going to get. He knew they were posers.

Don't be afraid to be on fire for the LORD. Don't be afraid to let your enthusiasm and excitement for His blessings, His love, and the hope of eternity radiate from every part of you. Not only will your attitude influence others for Christ, but it give you the assurance of knowing your Heavenly home is secure.

Tell at least three people this week just how happy you are that Jesus is your Savior.

Intentionally sing songs of praise to the LORD throughout the week. Sing in the shower, in the car, with someone you love, or while you are doing a chore or homework.

PRAYER

Father in heaven, I pray that my actions, my attitude, my facial expressions, and my words reflect the joy that comes from knowing and loving you. In your name I pray, amen.

Journal/Workspace

Week 32: Role Model

Remember your leaders, who spoke the word of God to you. Consider the outcome of their way of life and imitate their faith. (Hebrews 13:7)

APPLICATION

Hazel read Bible stories and patiently helped 3-year-old Dora and scores of other preschoolers glue cotton balls onto the sheep outline and color pictures of grapes, fish and bread, and make pop sickle stick people.

Joan tirelessly worked with a youth choir, taught music, and was the epitome of a godly woman. She was the 'real deal' and taught by example.

Judy was the 'big sister' one girl never had. She talked to her about relationships, modesty, purity, using her talents, and about the fact that she was fearfully and wonderfully made (Psalm 139).

Paul, helped his little brother deal with depression and helped him overcome the effects of being bullied.

Role models—those people whose faith is real and whose character is genuinely Christ-like—we all need them. Who are yours?

Write letters or send texts this week to those who have led you—whose faith and life are worth imitating. If they are no longer living, you can pay tribute to them on your social media, or visit their memorial place/graveside.

PRAYER

LORD, Thank you for giving me (fill in the blanks) to be an example of what it means to be like you. Thank you for their faith and their willingness to invest in my life. In your name I pray, amen.

Journal/Workspace

Week 33: Hope

Hope deferred makes the heart sick, but a desire fulfilled is a tree of life. (Proverbs 13:12)

APPLICATION

A young couple hoped for the chance to be parents. Day and night for five years they hoped with all their hearts…desperately, you might say…to wear the titles of "Dad" and "Mom". On the day they got the call to come to the hospital to meet the newborn son they would adopt, their hope was no longer being deferred. They were basking in the shade of their tree of life.

What are some things you have hoped for in your life? How did you feel when you got them? Did they meet or exceed your expectations? Or were you disappointed?

Hoping for things of this world brings temporary satisfaction at best. But when we hope for the things of Christ we will never be disappointed. We will experience lasting fulfillment and satisfaction. So take a few minutes to think about the things you are currently hoping for. As you read the daily verses this week, let them help you decide if you are hoping for things that will bring lasting fulfillment? If not, what can you hope for instead that will?

Day 1: Romans 15:13

Day 2: Isaiah 40:31

Day 3: Jeremiah 17:7

Day 4: Lamentations 3:24

Day 5: Luke 1:37

Day 6: Psalm 37:3-7

Day 7: 1st Peter 1:13

PRAYER

Father in heaven, I come to you asking that you make the longings of my heart the same as yours. And let those longing fill me with joy and satisfaction. In Jesus' name I pray, amen.

Journal/Workspace

Week 34: Reflection

You who are young, be happy while you are young, and let your heart give you joy in the days of your youth. Follow the ways of your heart and whatever your eyes see, but know that for all these things God will bring you into judgment. (Ecclesiastes 11:9)

APPLICATION

Solomon wrote these words near the end of his life. And what a life it had been! He had experienced the highest of highs and lowest of lows. He had anything a guy could possibly want and lots of it—including wisdom.

It was because of his wisdom that Solomon came to understand the truth in today's verse—that we will be judged for the way we live our life here on earth. That can be a scary thought, can't it? Especially if you are struggling with being able to comprehend and accept the saving grace of God that forgives our sins.

None of us will be able to stand blameless before God. But we can stand before Him knowing we are forgiven and living to please and honor Him.

Q: What would you say are the 'ways of your heart' you want to follow?

Q: Is your answer different today than it would have been at another time in your life? Why or why not?

Q: How does Solomon's advice make you feel?

PRAYER

LORD, Keep my heart and mind set on things that will not make me ashamed to stand before you to be judged someday. Make my heart like yours. In Jesus' name I pray, amen.

Journal/Workspace

Week 35: Rest

On the eighth day hold a closing special assembly and do no regular work. (Numbers 29:35)

APPLICATION

Throughout the books of the Law, God tells the people over and over again that there are certain times they are to rest. He also commands them to let the ground rest from growing crops and the animals rest from working. Rest is important. It replenishes the body. It allows the brain to slow down. It relieves physical pressures from our bones and joints. It 'forces' us to stop and take stock of our need for dependence on our maker.

Rest also does one other very important thing—it blocks out the noise and activity so that we can hear and see God without any distractions. In resting we grow in our intimacy with the Savior.

Set aside at least thirty minutes a day each day this week to rest. No work. No electronics. Nothing but you, peace and quiet, and the LORD.

PRAYER

Father, don't let me become too busy for you. Let me take the time to rest so that my body and my spirit can be refreshed. In the name of Jesus I pray, amen.

Journal/Workspace

Week 36: Cultivate

 *Blessed are those who hunger and thirst for righteousness, for they will be filled. (Matthew 5:6)*

APPLICATION

If you stop and think about it, most of the best things in life don't come without a fair amount of difficulty or unpleasantness.

Those delicious cucumbers and green beans we enjoy out of the garden have to lie in the dirt and mud for a while before they become edible. Our brains and bodies get tired and stressed from hours of thinking before we come up with a good idea.

Women who have given birth can certainly testify to the fact that pain is definitely a part of the process, but that it's worth it because of the overwhelming love and contentment having a child brings.

The blessing of being filled with righteousness, that is morally right, only happens when we give ourselves over to God in obedience. This isn't always easy and it doesn't happen without a fair amount of struggling. But, don't give up.

We don't mean to hold on to a bad habit. Often, we do it without thinking. Denying self can be painful, but the end-result of being filled with the righteousness of God and the hope of Heaven makes everything else seem empty.

What do you need to empty out of your life in order to let God's righteousness fill you completely? Throughout this week, think about these things. Pray about these things. What do you need to get rid of in order to start living a fuller life.

PRAYER

LORD, take away the sinful and worldly desires of my heart. Replace them with desire, courage, and commitment to be like you in all things. In your name I pray, amen.

Journal/Workspace

Week 37: Trust

 *"But LORD," Gideon asked, "how can I save Israel? My clan is the weakest in Manesseh, and I am the least in my family." The LORD answered, "I will be with you, and you will strike down all the Midianites together. (Judges 6:15-16)*

APPLICATION

Gideon was a 'nobody' in the eyes of his people. What's more, Gideon was a 'nobody' in his own eyes. But God knew better. Using Gideon, God gave Israel victory over the Midianites using just three-hundred men. Using Gideon, God destroyed the idols the Israelites were worshipping instead of God.

How was it possible for God to work through Gideon? In a word…trust. Gideon had to *trust* God to do the seemingly impossible. Gideon had to trust God to protect him. Gideon had to *trust* God to keep his word. And God did. Every single time.

You, too, can trust God. You can trust Him to keep every promise he made that is written in the Bible. God is the God of truth. He is the very essence of truth and honesty. God cannot lie. You will never be sorry when you put your trust in Him.

Try the following this week:

1: Trust God with your heart by writing out your thoughts and fears, then read them aloud to God.

2: Ask God to give you the courage to trust Him with everything in your life.

3: What is something you have always been afraid to do? Ask God to give you the courage to do it and then do it—trusting God to take away your fear.

PRAYER

God, give me courage to trust you and to trust in myself because I know you are with me. In Jesus' name I pray, amen.

Journal/Workspace

Week 38: Direction

I will instruct you and teach you in the way you should go; I will counsel you with my eye upon you. (Psalm 32:8)

APPLICATION

Have you ever played a game with someone who tried making the rules up as you went along? Or, have you ever tried to put something together without the instructions? Find your way to someplace new without directions? None of these things are much fun, are they?

Going direction-less wastes time and energy. It creates frustration and causes you to make mistakes—some of which can be very costly. But, we don't have to worry about being direction-less. God loves us too much and values our time and talents too much to leave us hanging. He doesn't want us to waste a single minute wondering what we are supposed to do or who we are in Him. So trust in Him to do it—follow the directions he gives you for your life. In doing so, you will never be lost or disappointed ever again.

Read the verse for each day and let them lead you as they are meant to.

Day 1: Psalm 37:23

Day 2: Isaiah 11:2

Day 3: Proverbs 16:1-2

Day 4: Psalm 94:12-14

Day 5: Psalm 90:12

Day 6: John 15:1-5

Day 7: Isaiah 6:8

PRAYER

God, show me the way you created me to go. Give me the faith I need to follow your directions without fail. In Jesus' name I pray, amen.

Journal/Workspace

Week 39: Changes

Do not think I have come to abolish the Law or the Prophets; I have not come to abolish them but to fulfill them. (Matthew 5:17)

APPLICATION

These are the words of Jesus. He was speaking to members of the Jewish race…the Israelites. They were living under the Mosaic Law. It was the Law God gave Moses to give to the Israelites approx. 1,600 years prior to Jesus' birth. So it is understandable that the people would be a bit hesitant and skeptical. It was all they had ever known. And now they were supposed to change? Yikes!

Change can be scary. But when the changes mean something better is in store for you, why wouldn't you change? The changes Jesus requires of us when we accept Him as our Savior can be intimidating and a bit scary. We can't be sure others will accept the change in us. We aren't sure we can change our spending habits and tithe like we are commanded to do. We aren't sure we can change the way we talk, give up sleeping in on Sunday mornings, or living with our boyfriend or girlfriend outside of marriage.

Are changes really necessary in our recovery? The answer is yes. We cannot live a worldly and sinful life and be obedient to Jesus at the same time (Matt 6:24).

Which of the following changes will you make beginning this week?

1: I will change my budget to tithe as I have been commanded by God to do.

2: I will change the way I respond to others.

3: I will change my habit of _____ so it no longer has control over me.

PRAYER

Father in heaven, Show me the changes I need to make in my life in order to be more like you—to reflect who you are to those around me. Give me the strength and desire to make these changes. In the name of Jesus I pray, amen.

Journal/Workspace

Week 40: Fellowship

And let us consider how we may spur one another on toward love and good deeds. (Hebrews 10:24)

APPLICATION

Irene and her husband, James, had been married for less than six months when he left to fight in Viet Nam. Three months later Irene received that dreaded telegram…James was dead. He was the love of her life. They had so many plans for a family and their future.

Irene never remarried. Instead, she put her heart, soul, body, and mind into serving God in the local church. Of all the things she did, though, teaching Sunday school was her favorite. For forty-five years Irene faithfully taught the third and fourth graders. For forty-five years she showered them with her Godly wisdom, love, special treats and gifts. She welcomed them into her home for parties, and recognized their accomplishments at school and other places. Irene's love and attention didn't stop when they left her class, though. If you were Irene's in class, you were Irene's for life. Dozens of young couples received "Irene quilts" as wedding gifts.

On Irene's sixty-fifth birthday she wondered if she should retire from teaching. Maybe the children needed someone younger, she thought. But, that evening her doorbell rang. Opening her door, Irene found forty students, parents, and former students shouting "Happy birthday!"

The party was just a little token of appreciation, they said, for all the things she had done to touch their lives. The party had been just what she needed to remind her that you are never too old to love, encourage, teach, and to fellowship.

Visit at least two people this week; spending time in fellowship and encouraging them in their faith.

PRAYER

LORD, Thank you for my family and for friends all over the world. Open my heart and eyes to different ways I can fellowship with them. In Jesus' name I pray, amen.

Journal/Workspace

Week 41: Self-Care

Do you not know that your bodies are temples of the Holy Spirit, who is in you, whom you have received from God? You are not your own; you were bought at a price. Therefore honor God with your bodies. (1 Corinthians 6:19)

APPLICATION

You've undoubtedly heard the slogans: "You are what you eat" and "Garbage in…Garbage out". The message behind both is that we should take care of our bodies and our minds. But we don't always do that, do we? Instead, we might overeat or starve or purge after eating. We might abuse our bodies with tobacco, alcohol, or drugs. Or, we may subject ourselves to abuse at the hands of another.

Jesus' death on the cross was a sacrifice for our sins—his body in exchange for ours. In other words, we are now free to present our bodies back to God as an expression of gratitude for the gift of salvation through Jesus' body on the cross. God deserves our best and that means we can take pride in ourselves.

Make it a point to do the things on this self-care check list before the week is over:

1: Treat yourself to a haircut, a manicure, and/or a new item of clothing.

2: Commit to taking a walk (or another form of exercise) at least three times this week to improve your circulation, your muscle tone, and your overall level of feeling good.

3: Memorize today's verse OR write it on post-it notes and place it somewhere so you can read it throughout the day.

PRAYER

LORD, I pray I will see my body the way you do—as a precious part of your creation. Please give me the confidence and desire to have a positive outlook on self-care and to treat my body and mind with love and respect. In Jesus' name I pray, amen.

Journal/Workspace

Week 42: Limits

If we deliberately keep on sinning after we have received the knowledge of the truth, no sacrifice for sins is left, but only a fearful expectation of judgment and of raging fire that will consume the enemies of God. (Hebrews 10:26-27)

APPLICATION

I once had someone say that reading these two verses made them feel threatened or even bullied. They said they didn't think it was right to try to scare someone into not sinning. These verses weren't meant to be threatening. Rather, they are God's warning to us to stay within the limits or boundaries he has set. God cares for us and gives us warning so we can be saved, not harmed. Think about it like this: When a parent says, "If you don't watch for traffic when you are riding your bike, I'm not going to allow you to ride it anymore," the parent isn't being a bully. He or she is setting limits in order to keep them safe and alive, which is exactly what God is doing with us in these two verses.

We all need limits. They provide us with a sense of security and structure which allows us to function optimally because we know what is expected of us.

If you continue in your addiction, what do you think will eventually happen? Would it be a consequence of what you do, or merely a punishment?

Read the verse for each day. Choose one (or more) to memorize.

Day 1: Revelation 14:12   Day 2: Galatians 6:7

Day 3: Mark 16:16   Day 4: John 14:6

Day 5: Matthew 7:21   Day 6: 1 John 1:8-10

Day 7: 2nd Timothy 1:7

PRAYER

LORD, open my eyes, ears, heart, and mind to the limits you've placed around me and help me live within them. In your son's name I pray, amen.

Journal/Workspace

Week 43: Anger

In your anger do not sin: Do not let the sun go down while you are still angry. (Ephesians 4:26)

APPLICATION

Please read this verse carefully. What do make of it? Do you see that it isn't a sin just to be angry—the problem is sinning *because* you are angry. There's a big difference between the two.

Jesus was angry when he walked into the Temple and saw people selling things for profit. Peter's tone was definitely angry on the Day of Pentecost when he was telling the people that they had murdered the Messiah a few weeks ago. Jesus' anger did not cause him to sin. He simply righted the wrong and went on. Peter's anger quickly turned to compassion and joy when the people asked what they needed to do to be saved from their sin…and obeyed.

You've undoubtedly experienced conflict in your life and you are undoubtedly going to experience more, which means you are going to be angry. When this happens, don't let the words and actions lead you into sin. Let this week's verse remind you to take the time to calmly and respectfully right the wrong (to whatever extent you can) and move on.

This week's assignment is to rid yourself of any anger you are harboring, not allowing you to sin.

1: Are you harboring any anger? If so, what is it and why?

2: What needs to be done for you to let these things go?

3: Write out a plan of action for getting rid of your anger and ask God to help you.

4: Pray the prayer below before you go to sleep each night.

PRAYER

God, thank you for showing me that it is okay to be angry when anger is justified as long as my anger is Godly and as long as I don't let it lead me into sin. Help me be discerning in when I should and shouldn't be angry. In Jesus' name I pray, amen.

Journal/Workspace

Week 44: Fear

 *Do not be afraid of those who kill the body but cannot kill the soul. Rather, be afraid of the One who can destroy both soul and body in hell. (Matthew 10:28)*

APPLICATION

When Connie was diagnosed an aggressive form of cancer she only a few months left to live. When she shared the news with her best friend, her friend tearfully asked, "Are you afraid to die?"

Connie smiled, slowly shook her head, and said, "No, I'm really not—and here's why. My Aunt Wanda was with me at the hospital the night Dad died. In those last minutes before he died, Aunt Wanda took my hand and said, 'Connie, don't worry about your dad. There are a lot worse things in life than dying.' As I sat there watching him take his last few breaths, I realized she was right. There are a lot worse things than dying—dying without knowing Jesus, for one."

There are plenty of things in this world that can make us fearful. But no matter how scary, painful, sad, or evil these things are, God is bigger, mightier, and more powerful. With God on our side we truly do not have to be afraid.

This week, ask a family member or friend what they might be afraid of. Pray with them; asking God to help them not be afraid.

PRAYER

Father in Heaven, I know you are all-powerful and mighty. I know you can defeat anything that scares me. Help me put my trust in you and not be afraid. In the name of Jesus I pray, amen.

Journal/Workspace

Week 45: Gratitude

Give thanks to the Lord, for he is good. His love endures forever. (Psalm 136:1)

APPLICATION

Scientists say that gratitude has positive impacts on health and can actually slow down the aging process. Well, that's something to be grateful for, right? But what motivates our gratitude? The Bible tells us to bring forth the message of God through praises of gratitude (Col 3:16).

See what happens when you open your heart afresh to the Lord, moving beyond the normal, the canned, the almost obligatory phrases of praise and worship, where you truly begin to 'magnify Him with thanksgiving' (Psalm 69:30)…see if expressing gratitude to the Lord doesn't 'magnify' Him in your eyes, increasing your depth perception of this One who knows your name, counts the hairs on your head, and manifests His love for you with one blessing after another. See if the practice of intentional gratitude doesn't transport you even nearer to Him—not just where your faith can believe it but where your heart can sense it. Thanksgiving puts us in God's living room. It paves the way to His presence.

- Nancy DeMoss Wolgemuth, Family Life

Write thank you notes to at least five people this week—thanking them for being your friend or loving family member and/or for something they have done or given you recently.

PRAYER

Father in heaven, Thank you for all you do for me. Thank you for the blessings of family, friends, and all that you have provided for me. Most of all, though, thank you for the sacrifice of Jesus that gives me the hope of heaven. In his name I pray these things, amen.

Journal/Workspace

Week 46: Thanksgiving

Do not be anxious about anything, but in every situation, by prayer and petition, with thanksgiving, present your requests to God. (Philippians 4:6).

APPLICATION

In the book of Philippians Paul is trying to convey an important message. That we need not worry. He reminds us to give thanksgiving when we ask God for something. We should not forget what he has given us already. We need not worry about the outcome of our prayer, only that we give thanks in our petition. It is up to God what happens. This is why we need not worry. God is in control!

Try these thanksgiving plans this week:

Day 1: Talk to God about what you are thankful for today.

Day 2: Tell someone close to you something you are thankful for.

Day 3: What new petition do you need to bring to God? Talk to Him about it today.

Day 4: As you prepare to eat your meal, present an extended thanksgiving to God.

Day 5: Think about what you were thankful for today. Tell someone close to you about it.

Day 6: How does anxiety associate with addiction? What are some things that have potential to create anxiety for you? Talk to God about anxiety. Ask God to remind you of things you can be thankful for and replace any anxiety with thanksgiving

Day 7: Attend church; or minister to the poor at a food kitchen; or visit a shut in and remind yourself what you are thankful for.

PRAYER

Thanks be to God, the maker of Heaven and Earth. Lord, as I work on my action plan, give me the strength and courage to see it through, amen.

Journal/Workspace

Week 47: Relationships

 *Iron sharpens iron, and one man sharpens another. (Proverbs 27:17)*

APPLICATION

Jesus took a few men and changed their reputations from uneducated fishermen, hated tax-collector, pessimist, and violent activist (just to name a few) to that of being a Christ-follower.

The same violent activist, whose name was Saul (but changed to Paul), helped change the reputations of countless people from worldly sinners to Christians.

How did Jesus and Paul do it? By establishing and building relationships with them—talking to them, listening to them, experiencing life together.

It's true. A person is known by the company he/she keeps. So ask yourself what your relationships say about you?

Take some time each day this week to read the verses listed below; letting them guide you in making decisions to make sure your relationships are healthy for you both physically and spiritually.

Day 1: John 15:13   Day 2: Proverbs 17:17

Day 3: 1 Corinthians 15:33 Day 4: Hebrews 10:24-25

Day 5: Job 6:14   Day 6: Luke 6:31

Day 7: 1 Corinthians 13:1-13

PRAYER

God, Thank you for the healthy and positive relationships in my life. I pray that I will show my gratitude by giving back what they give to me. Let me also be discerning and tactfully remove myself from the relationships that are not healthy for me. In your son's name I pray, amen.

Journal/Workspace

Week 48: Responsibility

The man said, "The woman you put here with me-she gave me some fruit from the tree, and I ate it." (Genesis 3:12)

APPLICATION

Adam was quick to blame both God and Eve for his disobedience…his sin. He blamed God for giving Eve to him and Eve for giving him the fruit. In both instances Adam was the recipient. He was given someone and something. But what Adam failed to admit was that *he* took what he was offered. He didn't own up to his responsibility for his role in what happened.

You and you alone have control over your thoughts and actions. Blaming others for your circumstances is irresponsible. Blaming others also puts a huge roadblock across your path; making it impossible to move forward. Don't give someone else the power to decide what you do and say, or how far you grow. Do the responsible thing and become one with the One who made you…God.

Think about the following:

Q: Who and/or what do I blame for my problems?

Q: How has blaming these people/things affected my life?

Q: What do I need to do to be able to accept responsibility for my actions?

Q: How will doing so change my attitude and my situation?

PRAYER

God, Thank you for loving me even when I don't feel very loveable. Thank you, also, for giving me your Word to teach me that I need to take responsibility for who I am and what I do. Help me do this and help me let go of the resentment and blame I feel toward others. In the name of Jesus I pray, amen.

Journal/Workspace

Week 49: Christmas Time

The virgin will conceive and give birth to a son, and they will call Him Immanuel (which means "God with us") (Matthew 1:23).

APPLICATION

Christmastime is a celebration of the birth of Jesus. The season can also be embedded with various stressors, capitalism, and busyness. These distractions, not only at Christmastime, but throughout the year, can keep us from our true connection with God. Staying connected to Jesus, having that true "God with is," reality, requires our dedication to that, as well as some other principles. \

One of these principles is not letting the capitalism of Christmas side track us; remembering that we cannot buy love, that the memories of Christmas really come from loving each other and not from buying each other material things. If giving a gift is a token of your love for someone, so be it, but remember not to let that dictate the reason for Christmas.

Finally, how do we keep Christ in Christmas? What does it take to really feel "God with us"? How do you keep Christ in the center of your recovery? Use the following to help you keep Christ in your recovery:

Using you journal/workspace, make a list of things you will do that will keep you connected and centered this week. For each item, be specific, and include a date/time for which it will be accomplished.

PRAYER

During this season, Lord it is so easy to get distracted and to lose sight of you. Christmas really is about reflecting on your birth and the true meaning is that you want to be connected to us. Help me to keep close to you and in that leaving no space for my addiction to take control, amen.

Journal/Workspace

Week 50: Worship

 *Jesus answered, "It is written: 'Worship the Lord your God and serve Him only." (Luke 4:8)*

APPLICATION

How do you worship; who do you worship? John 4:23 tell us that true worshipers will worship the Father in the Spirit and in truth. Worship is obedience to the Spirit of Christ, not to mere rules (Mark 7:7). Worship is really about being in the Spirit, listening to God, walking in His ways (truth), and embraced in his grace and presence. This worship leads to joy (Luke 24:52). Addiction on the other hand is the worship of substances, impulses, temporal physical pleasures, or other vices. But, this form of worship only leads to destruction (Gal 6: 7-8).

"…I'm coming back to the heart of worship…and it's all about you, Jesus…"

-Matt Redman

Prepare your heart for worship this week by watching (for the lyrics) and listening to "The Heart of Worship" by Matt Redman found here at: https://www.youtube.com/watch?v=Y0a9T0UtJBQ

PRAYER

Father, my flesh is weak, I often feel compelled to worship the lusts of the flesh rather than the Spirit. Help me Lord to embrace your presence so that your joy shines in me. In the name of your son I pray, amen.

Journal/Workspace

Week 51: Joy

I have told you this so that my joy be in you and that your joy may be complete (John 15:11)

APPLICATION

Jesus's joy came as a result of following his Father's leadership, obeying his commands. Following God's framework for living ultimately produces joy. To remain in God's truths brings about joy. As we see in John 15, it is His love for us that produces this joy. How often have we taken for granted God's love for us? How many times have we disobeyed His commands? Recovery is a process of engaging in God's love and following his commands. It is this road that we find true recovery and relief of our past and the light for our futures.

Ponder these questions this week:

1) What commands are you not following that are dampening your spirits and bringing unhappiness?

2) What do you need to do to obey those commands?

3) What will you do to accomplish this?

PRAYER

Lord, please make my joy complete. May I gain the strength I need to obey your commands and living according to your ways and principles. I need you and want to feel your love that brings the greatest joy of all.

Journal/Workspace

Week 52: Needs

And my God will meet all your needs according to the riches of his glory in Christ Jesus. (Philippians 4:19)

APPLICATION

The widow of Zarephath had just enough flour and oil for each day—even though she used what was there each morning to make the day's bread. For forty years the Israelites awoke to find a fresh supply of manna and quail. One boy's small lunch of fish and bread became enough for thousands.

We are loved by our father, God. His love is a love that will not disappoint and will not fail to supply our needs. All we have to do is ask Him in faith, knowing he hears and answers our prayers. Like any good parent, our needs are of great concern to God and he will not leave them unmet.

God meets our needs in a number of ways. One of those ways is through other people. Be the hands and feet of our heavenly father this week by meeting the needs of two or three people. Some suggestions could include: Mowing an elderly person's lawn, or doing a task for them. Fixing a meal for someone who is sick or pregnant. Leaving a bag or two of groceries on the doorstep of a family or individual in need. Donating clothes or gift cards to a family or individual who is having money troubles. Visiting someone in a nursing home who rarely sees anyone but the staff and other residents (see also James 1:27; Matthew 25:45, Matthew 6:3; Luke 11:10).

PRAYER

God, Thank you for your constant love and care. The joy and relief that comes from knowing you will always meet my needs is amazing. Help me share this joy with others by being your willing servant. In Jesus' name I pray, amen.

Journal/Workspace

Journal/Workspace

Journal/Workspace

Journal/Workspace

Journal/Workspace

Journal/Workspace

Journal/Workspace

Enjoy other Workbooks by this author:

*"The Addictions Workbook:
101 Practical Exercises for Individuals and Group (3rd ed.)"*

Order at:
www.createspace.com/6551286

www.ingramcontent.com/pod-product-compliance
Lightning Source LLC
LaVergne TN
LVHW081358060426
835510LV00016B/1891

THE STAGES OF CHANGE
WORKBOOK

James E. Phelan

"The Stages of Change Workbook"

Order at
www.createspace.com/4575536